GOING VEGETARIAN

A HEALTHY GUIDE TO MAKING THE SWITCH

by Dana Meachen Rau

COMPASS POINT BOOKS
a capstone imprint

Compass Point Books
1710 Roe Crest Drive
North Mankato, MN 56003

Acknowledgments

Special thanks to Hanako Agresta, Ashley Case,
Alyssa Moskites, Kimberly Parker, and Jenna Sadecki
for sharing their stories with me.

Editor: Jeni Wittrock
Designer: Sarah Bennett
Media Researcher: Marcie Spence
Production Specialist: Danielle Ceminsky

Library of Congress Cataloging-in-Publication Data
Rau, Dana Meachen, 1971–
  Going vegetarian : a healthy guide to making the switch /
by Dana Meachen Rau.
     p. cm.
  Summary: "Describes the benefits, challenges, and steps to switching to a vegetarian diet"—Provided by publisher.
  Includes bibliographical references and index.
  ISBN 978-0-7565-4522-2 (library binding)—ISBN 978-0-7565-4530-7 (paperback)
  1. Vegetarian children—Juvenile literature. 2. Vegetarianism—Juvenile literature. 3. Nutrition—Juvenile literature. I. Title.
  RJ206.R28 2012
  613.2'62—dc23   2011040836

Image Credits: Alamy Images: Andia, 18-19, Nordicphotos, 13, PhotoEdit, 20; Capstone Studio: Karon Dubke, cover, 10, 11, 25, 39, 51, 59; Corbis: Chev Wilkinson/cultura, 7, Thomas A. Kelly, 47; iStockphoto: GeorgePeters, 43, Neustockimages, 45 (right), Rehlik, 23, Suljo, 22; Shutterstock: Andrea Skjold, 49 (right), arbalet, 19 (right), ARENA Creative, 30, ARTBOXCOM, 34, auremar, 38, BalazsT, 57, Daniel Taeger, 8, Dmitriy Shironosov, 53, Elena Elisseeva, 29, Elena Schweitzer, 33, Elke Dennis, 48-49, Evgenia Sh, 31, Jonathan Feinstein, 44-45, Kamila Panasiuk, 14; Li Xiang, 15; LiteChoices, 16, Monkey Business Images, 5, 55, Nadezhda Sundikova, 58, Nattika, 48 (left), paparazzit, 41, Picsfive, 36, pixelpeter, 24, sarah2, 32, Sundebo, 18 (left), Supri Suharjoto, 27, Tischenko Irina, 35, urosr, 17, Valeriy Velikov, 50, william casey, 42

Visit Compass Point Books on the Internet at *www.capstonepub.com*.

Printed in the United States of America in Stevens Point, Wisconsin.
072013   007593R

CONTENTS

CHAPTER ONE

MEATLESS MEALS

THE SCHOOL CAFETERIA BUZZES WITH THE CHATTER OF FRIENDS. Some kids wait in the long lunch line to pick up a cheeseburger from the grill. One girl snags a plate of chicken nuggets. A boy pays for a ham sandwich at the checkout.

But not Jenna. This seventh-grader is already at her table, unpacking her lunch from home. She brings it every day because she's decided to go vegetarian. The cafeteria doesn't offer many meatless choices for her.

"My friends call me crazy," Jenna says, "but they get it." She eats her Greek yogurt, cheese sticks, and fruit while her friends eat from the school lunch menu. It's not easy to eat differently from everyone else. But Jenna's not alone. In fact, on the other side of the same cafeteria, Hanako is unpacking her vegetarian lunch too—peanut butter and a bagel. Her friends support her choice to go vegetarian. "Other than everyone joking around," she says, "they respect my decision."

More and more teenagers are deciding to switch to meals without meat. Are you thinking of going vegetarian too?

VARIETY OF VEGETARIANS

Americans eat a lot of meat. According to the United States Department of Agriculture, we consumed a total of 26.9 billion pounds of beef in 2009 alone. Check out what's on an American menu: bacon, sausage, or ham for breakfast, deli meat sandwiches for lunch, steak tips, chicken breast, pork chops, or barbeque ribs for dinner. Summer picnic tables are stacked with hot dogs and hamburgers. Chilly winters bring beef stew or chicken soup. Meat is at the center of many meals.

Some people have had enough meat. They've decided to go vegetarian. Not all vegetarians follow the same guidelines. Some have decided to remove all types of meat from their diets. That means red meat, poultry, fish, and shellfish. Some still eat meat once in a while, and others don't count fish as meat.

Chicken consumption has been on the increase since the 1970s. The national average has climbed from 40.2 pounds per person in 1970 to 86.5 pounds per person in 2007.

Move over, meat! Vegetables and even fruits are tasty cooked on the grill too.

Many still eat animal products, such as eggs and dairy. Vegans take vegetarianism all the way—they don't eat animal products of any kind. That means no meat, eggs, dairy, or any other product that comes from an animal, such as gelatin, lard, or honey.

IT'S UP TO YOU

Making the choice to go vegetarian is a personal one. You can define your own rules and decide what to cut out of your diet. Are there foods that you'll miss if you go vegetarian? You can probably find a vegetarian alternative. But if not, it's up to you where you want to draw the line.

Alyssa became a vegan when she was 17. She's strict about not consuming animal products. "If I ever broke the rules," she says, "it was by accident." But the rules she made for herself aren't a problem. "There's nothing that I miss."

Alyssa has noticed that some of her friends have tried vegetarianism "because they think that it's cool." But she doesn't think that's the right reason. "You have to know what you're getting yourself into," she says.

What are you getting yourself into? Keep reading to find out what it takes to go vegetarian.

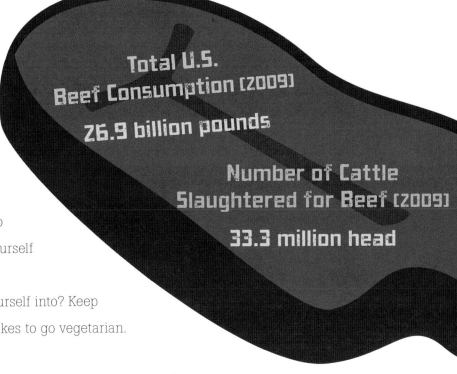

Total U.S.
Beef Consumption [2009]
26.9 billion pounds

Number of Cattle
Slaughtered for Beef [2009]
33.3 million head

Types of Vegetarians

ovo-lacto vegetarian:
no red meat, poultry, or fish / eats eggs and dairy

pesci-vegetarian:
no red meat or poultry / eats fish

ovo vegetarian:
no red meat, poultry, fish, or dairy / eats eggs

flexitarian:
eats meat occasionally

lacto vegetarian:
no red meat, poultry, fish, or eggs / eats dairy

vegan:
eats no animal products of any kind

This book is geared toward ovo-lacto vegetarians.

PESTO PASTA

Are you thinking of "going green" at dinnertime? Try this green and meatless meal that's easy, fun, and delicious! (Makes about 1 cup of sauce. Serves 4 to 6 people.)

Ingredients

1 packed cup fresh basil leaves

2 packed cups baby spinach

¼ cup olive oil

⅓ cup fresh parmesan cheese

¼ cup chopped walnuts

1 clove fresh garlic

Salt and pepper to taste

1 pound whole wheat pasta

1 cup small, round fresh mozzarella balls (called ciliegine), cut in half

1 cup cherry tomatoes, cut in half

Steps

Blend the basil, spinach, oil, parmesan, walnuts, and garlic in a blender or food processor until creamy. Add salt and pepper to taste.

Cook the pasta according to package directions. Drain.

In a large bowl, combine the pasta and the sauce, tossing well until the pasta is coated.

Serve pasta in bowls. Top each serving with fresh mozzarella and tomatoes. Garnish with thin-cut basil, if desired.

You can serve this meal cold as a pasta salad too.

Let's Eat

CHAPTER TWO

WHY VEGETARIAN?

IT CAN BE HARD TO BE A VEGETARIAN WHEN AMERICAN MEALS ARE OFTEN CENTERED ON MEAT.
In other countries, such as India, vegetables or lentils often make up the main meal. Indians who practice Hinduism don't eat beef because they believe cows are sacred. The Muslims in India do not eat pork. Vegetarianism is deeply rooted in Indian culture. Some other world religions and cultures also have rules regarding meat consumption.

Most kids practice the same beliefs as their parents. The adults in your household are probably the ones who purchase and cook the food. If they eat meat, you probably eat meat too. You may not have a choice in the matter. The same is true for teens with vegetarian parents. If you asked them why they're vegetarians, they may say it's because their parents are.

Religion or cultural upbringing are only two reasons people leave out meat and turn to a vegetarian diet. Here are other reasons why people make the switch.

GREATER GOOD

A food chain is the path energy travels through an ecosystem. Light from the sun and nutrients in the soil give plants energy. The plants give that energy to animals that eat them. If humans eat the animals, they get energy from those animals. Some vegetarians believe that if we skip the animal step and eat plants instead, we can get more energy from our food.

Besides energy, many vegetarians eat lower on the food chain in order to eat more healthfully. Many experts agree that going vegetarian is a healthy move. The American Dietetic Association, a group of food and nutrition professionals, has officially stated that eating vegetarian is a healthful lifestyle choice.

Going vegetarian can also be a step toward solving world hunger. Today the world population is 7 billion people, and it's growing every minute. More than 900 million people are considered undernourished.

According to the USDA Foreign Agricultural Service, in 2007 more than 50 percent of the total grain consumed in the United States was fed to livestock. Vegetarians believe that if you took the acres and acres devoted to livestock, and grew crops for human consumption instead, you could feed a lot more people. Eating lower on the food chain would mean more available food for the world.

According the the USDA's Natural Resources Conservation Service, more than 27 percent of privately owned land in the continental U.S. is range and pastureland.

Cattle and domestic livestock eat in pastures (above) or in feedlots (left).

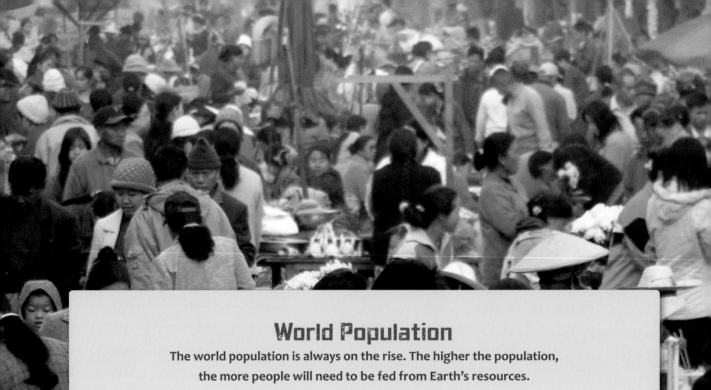

World Population

The world population is always on the rise. The higher the population, the more people will need to be fed from Earth's resources.

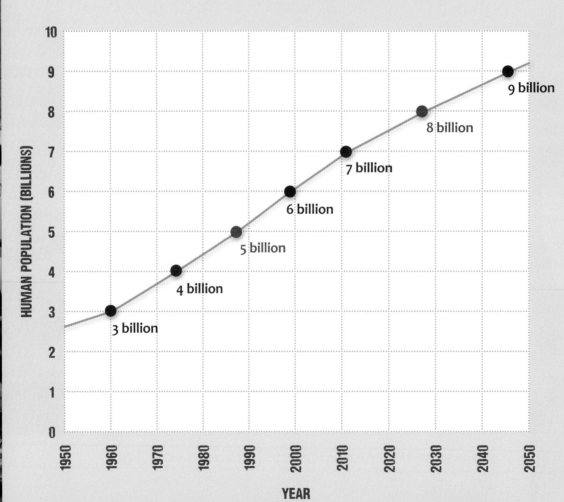

Graph — World Population

HUMAN POPULATION (BILLIONS) vs YEAR

- 3 billion (1960)
- 4 billion (1975)
- 5 billion (1987)
- 6 billion (1999)
- 7 billion (2011)
- 8 billion (2027)
- 9 billion (2046)

AIR AND LAND ISSUES

In addition to helping feed the world's people, some vegetarians believe that their choices help Earth itself.

You've probably heard debates over climate change. Too many harmful gases in Earth's atmosphere can affect climate over time. Electrical power, transportation, industry, and agriculture create an excess of dangerous gases that enter the air. According to the United Nations Food and Agriculture Organization, the handling of livestock greatly contributes to gas emissions. They have stated that "livestock are one of the most significant contributors to today's most serious environmental problems."

As livestock digest food, they release gases in their manure. But gases are also released by the production of fertilizers to grow feed crops, the production of the feed, the production of animal meat, and the transportation of processed and refrigerated animal products.

Too much grazing presents problems too. Herds of animals trample the ground and cause land erosion. Overgrazing can cause desertification—land becomes completely unusable, for animals, crops, or people.

Forests around the world are being destroyed to create grazing ground for cattle.

17

WATER ISSUES

Livestock waste is sometimes used as manure to fertilize crops. Excess waste, however, is kept in big waste lagoons. These lagoons can seep into local water systems and cause pollution.

Manure also contains chemicals from the fertilizers and pesticides used to grow the crops that feed animals. This gets into the groundwater too. Groundwater provides our drinking water. It feeds the nearby waterways. Contaminants can destroy the organisms that live there.

Livestock also account for a huge use of water. Animals need to drink it. Water is used to clean equipment. Mostly, though, it's

used to irrigate animal feed crops. It takes a lot more water to produce one pound of beef than it takes to produce one pound of grain.

Check out what's happening in the ocean too. The huge nets of fishing boats often scoop up everything in their path, not just fish to sell, but also endangered species. The nets can destroy coral reefs and other underwater environments. Overfishing can wipe an animal out of an ecosystem altogether. Because animals of an area are closely linked in a food chain, removing one species affects many of the species that live there.

Freshwater Use in the World

IRRIGATION → 70%
INDUSTRY → 22%
DOMESTIC USE → 8%

Fish are the only wild animals still hunted on a large scale, and their numbers are rapidly declining.

Limited space and specialized feed make factory farm chickens quickly grow large.

Chickens raised for meat are called broilers. According to USDA reports, American farmers raised and slaughtered more than 36 billion broiler chickens in 2010.

THE COST TO ANIMALS

Food may seem to just appear at the grocery store, but that's obviously not where it came from. And the cost may be more than just the money we pay for it.

Many vegetarians are concerned with how animals are raised, treated, and ultimately slaughtered so we can have meat on our tables. That's how Ashley feels. She turned vegetarian when she was 14. "Vegetarianism has made me realize how little people know about what they're eating," she says. "Humans view themselves as higher than everything else on Earth. Does that give us the right to slaughter everything in our path? We are animals too."

Industries create a supply of a product in response to customer demand. Because Americans eat so much meat, the food industry needs to supply a lot. This high demand results in farms that run like factories. They are called CAFOs (concentrated animal feeding operations). They are also known as factory farms.

So how does a "chicken factory" work? Chickens raised for meat are called broilers. Farmers keep thousands of them crowded in huge sheds. If the chickens had lots of room to run around, they might lose weight, and farmers want their chickens to weigh more, not less. Broiler chickens have also been bred to develop huge breasts—the white meat that customers want most. Sometimes, though, the chickens grow too heavy for their legs to support them, and they might not be able to walk at all.

Iowa, North Carolina, and Minnesota are the top three pork-producing states in the U.S.

Hogs raised for pork may also live in crowded indoor conditions. Farmers keep nursing sows in tiny stalls called farrowing crates. In these tight quarters, a mother pig might roll onto her piglets by mistake. Many crates are made to immobilize the sow. Metal bars keep her lying on her side at all times.

Cows don't graze on their natural diet of grass in a field. Instead, at CAFOs farmers feed their cows corn in outdoor feedlots. With so many cows in such a small space, they trample the ground and stand in thick waste. It can get on their fur and even into their feed.

Farmers want to fatten their animals as fast as possible. Along with constant feeding, they may inject the animals with growth hormones. Hormones help animals grow bigger faster and increase milk production in dairy cows. Farmers are also concerned with disease. When animals are crowded together, diseases spread easily. So farmers give their animals regular doses of antibiotics.

Conditions on large farms are unnatural for animals that are social creatures and need room to roam. Some smaller farms make an effort to raise their animals in a less stressful, more natural atmosphere. They may allow their cows to graze on grass in a pasture. They may give their chickens and pigs ample room and treat them more like animals than products. You may see labels on meat that say "free range" or "pasture raised" to tell customers how the animals have been treated. But these labels can be misleading. Large farms may adhere to

Organic Food

Another way to show compassion for the world—go organic! Conventional farming uses synthetic pesticides and fertilizers to grow crops. They can cause harm to the soil and surrounding environment. Organic farmers grow their produce in more natural ways. They rotate crops to put nutrients into the soil or compost plant scraps as fertilizer instead. They may use natural predators or approved organic pesticides to solve any insect problems.

Some—but not all—free-range farms give turkeys more room to roam.

Slabs of beef move along an assembly line. Livestock are slaughtered when they are about 5 or 6 months old.

government regulations for using these labels, but their treatment of animals may be similar to other factory farms. For example, even though a "cage free" chicken may not be kept in a cage, it still may be crowded with other chickens in a shed.

From the factory farm, animals are shipped to a slaughterhouse where they are stunned, hung, and carved into meat. The conditions are often dangerous for workers, who must work quickly, using knives on an assembly line.

A smaller farm might slaughter its animals in a way that causes them the least pain and stress. But people who have become vegetarians because of their concern for animals are opposed to killing these creatures for food, no matter how well they are treated before slaughter.

BLACK BEAN BURGER

Does no meat mean no burgers? Of course not! Vegan burgers are healthy and packed with flavor. (makes four burgers)

Ingredients

2 tablespoons olive oil, divided

1 cup grated zucchini (about 1 small)

1 cup grated carrot

¼ cup chopped onion

1 cup frozen corn

1 14-ounce can black beans, drained and rinsed

1 cup panko breadcrumbs

½ teaspoon smoked paprika

Salt and pepper to taste

Steps

In a large skillet, heat 1 tablespoon of olive oil on medium high. Add the zucchini, carrot, onion, and corn to the pan. Sauté for about 5 minutes until veggies soften.

Pulse the black beans in a food processor until pasty but still chunky (or mash with the back of a fork). Place in a large bowl.

Add the cooked veggies to the bean bowl. Add the breadcrumbs, paprika, salt, and pepper. Combine well.

With your hands, form the mixture into four patties. Refrigerate until ready to cook.

In a large skillet, heat 1 tablespoon of olive oil on medium. Cook the patties about 3 to 4 minutes a side or until warmed through.

CHAPTER THREE

KNOW YOUR NUTRIENTS

BEFORE JENNA BECAME A VEGETARIAN HER FAMILY "ATE MEAT PRETTY MUCH EVERY NIGHT." She never really liked meat, and so dinner often included an argument. When Jenna turned 11, she told her mother she wanted to become a vegetarian.

Jenna's mom made her do her research. Jenna filled 10 notebook pages with information about healthy eating, and how she could transition to a meatless diet while still getting the nutrients she needed. She learned more about food than she ever knew before she decided to give up meat.

Going vegetarian doesn't mean passing on the burger and just eating more French fries (potatoes are vegetables, right?). On the flip side, it's not just about eating salad all the time either. It's about variety. And vegetarians have lots of choices.

THE NUTRIENTS YOU NEED

Your body needs five basic nutrients: carbohydrates, protein, fat, vitamins, and minerals. Carbohydrates are the sugars and starches your body uses for energy. Complex carbohydrates take time for your body to break down, and simple carbohydrates can burn as energy right away. Fiber found in carbohydrates keeps your digestive system running well.

Proteins are made of amino acids, which are the building blocks your body uses to grow and repair itself. Your body makes some of these amino acids, but it has to get others—called essential amino acids—from your food.

Fat plays an important role in building body tissues, keeping you warm, and protecting your organs. Omega-3 fatty acids are among the good kinds. But saturated fats that are solid at room temperature (such as the fat found in meat) are not.

Vitamins and minerals help your body do specific tasks. Vitamin C helps you fight off colds. Vitamin A helps your eyesight. The mineral calcium builds your bones, and the mineral iron helps bring oxygen to your cells.

Step up to the counter and look at all the foods you have to choose from to feed your body's needs.

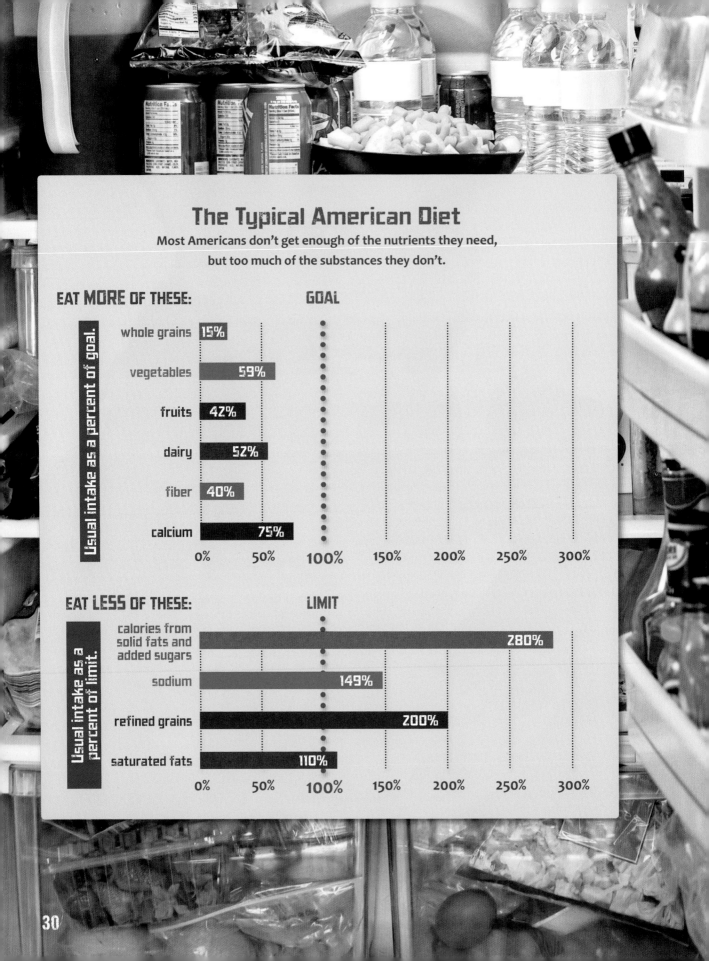

The Typical American Diet

Most Americans don't get enough of the nutrients they need,
but too much of the substances they don't.

EAT MORE OF THESE:
GOAL

Usual intake as a percent of goal.

whole grains	15%
vegetables	59%
fruits	42%
dairy	52%
fiber	40%
calcium	75%

0% 50% 100% 150% 200% 250% 300%

EAT LESS OF THESE:
LIMIT

Usual intake as a percent of limit.

calories from solid fats and added sugars	280%
sodium	149%
refined grains	200%
saturated fats	110%

0% 50% 100% 150% 200% 250% 300%

GREAT GRAINS

Grains are a major source of carbohydrates, and many of the foods you eat contain grain. The oatmeal or cereal you had for breakfast, the bread or tortilla for lunch, and the pasta or rice you have with dinner. Corn, wheat, rice, flax, oats, barley, and bulgur are grains. The closer they are to their natural state—which means whole grains as opposed to refined grains—the more nutritional value they have. "Refined" means that the food has had some of its nutrients stripped away in order to make it white, such as white bread and white rice.

LOTS OF LEGUMES

Have you ever heard of a legume? It's just a fancy word for beans, peas, and lentils. Legumes are plant-based proteins, and also sources of carbohydrates and vitamins. They are filling alternatives to meat (and some even have a "meaty" taste).

There may even be more types of legumes than there are kinds of meat! Lentils, chick peas, black beans, kidney beans, white beans, navy beans, black-eyed peas, split green peas, and soybeans are just a few of the many varieties.

Soybeans are made into many vegetarian alternatives, including soy milk and other dairylike products. Soy is also made into tofu, tempeh, and meat substitutes.

EGGS AND MILK

As an ovo-lacto vegetarian, you may eat dairy and egg products,
both good protein sources. Eggs can be scrambled, fried, and
baked into many dishes and treats. Dairy foods include milk, hard
and soft cheese, cottage cheese, and yogurt. Dairy foods also have
the additional advantage of being packed with calcium.

Vitamin B12 is an important vitamin your body needs.
It's found in meat, but hard to get from plant foods. You
can get B12 from milk and eggs. But if you've cut out
all animal products, you may
need to add a supplement to
your diet, or eat foods fortified
with B12.

NUTS FOR NUTS (AND SEEDS!)

Nuts and seeds are super foods, packed with lots of nutrients, including carbohydrates, protein, fat, vitamins, and minerals. You can eat a handful of them as a snack, sprinkle them on salads and cereal, bake them in cookies, or plan a whole meal around them.

Get the mineral calcium from almonds. Get iron from cashews, pine nuts, or pumpkin seeds. Find vitamin E in sunflower seeds, almonds, and hazelnuts. You can get the healthy omega-3 fatty acids that are found in fish from flax and walnuts instead.

Top 10 Protein-Packed Nuts

type of seed or nut	grams of protein (in one ounce)
peanut	7
pine nut	7
pumpkin seed	7
almond	6
hemp seed	6
pistachio	6
sunflower seed	6
flax seed	5
sesame seed	5
walnut	4

FRUITS AND VEGGIES

Fruit holds the simple sugars that your body can turn into energy. Starchy vegetables, such as potatoes, peas, and beans, are vitamin-packed sources of carbohydrates. Fruits and veggies also contain healthy fiber.

Find iron in dried fruit and spinach. Calcium comes in dark green vegetables, such as broccoli and kale. Good fats hide in avocadoes and olives. Yellow and orange vegetables, such as sweet potatoes and pumpkin, have extra beta-carotene. Try to eat a rainbow of fruits and vegetables to get the best variety of vitamins.

A HEALTHY MOVE

Vegetarians replace meat with a huge variety of options. They believe that by removing meat from their plates, and instead filling them with legumes, grains, eggs, low-fat dairy, nuts, seeds, fruits, and vegetables, they are giving their bodies a healthy advantage. Experts agree and have proven this fact in many medical studies.

Meat is a major source of saturated fat and cholesterol. These substances are closely tied to many health problems, such as heart disease, high blood pressure, diabetes, obesity, and some cancers. By cutting out meat, you will have a much lower risk for

Pass right by the meat counter to all the other departments your grocery store has to offer.

developing these problems. By replacing fat-filled protein with plant proteins, you benefit from the fiber, complex carbohydrates, and vitamins and minerals not found in meat.

Vegetarians don't have to worry about eating the traces of the hormones and antibiotics that get into an animal's meat. The dangerous bacteria E.coli that can get into the meat from an animal's waste is rarely a problem for vegetarians.

Vegetarians who cut out fish and shellfish don't have to worry about the toxins and dangerous metals often found in water-dwelling creatures. Metals such as lead and mercury, and farm and industrial waste make their way into our groundwater and then to our waterways. Animals absorb these dangerous substances. Larger fish have high levels of toxins because they eat smaller fish that absorbed toxins too.

After Jenna researched vegetarianism, her mom insisted that Jenna let her doctor in on the news. That's a great idea. A doctor can make sure you're getting the right nutrients, no matter what your diet. As a teenager you have to feed your body the nutrients it needs. After all, you want to be your best.

I Can't Eat That!

There are other reasons why some people avoid certain foods—allergies. These eight foods are responsible for 90 percent of food allergies:

peanuts   eggs   wheat

milk

soy   shellfish

tree nuts   fish

If you have allergies, no matter what food choices you make, be sure to read ingredient labels and make responsible and safe choices.

An Unhealthy Epidemic

According to the National Health and Nutrition Examination Survey, 17 percent of the current generation of children and teens in the United States are considered obese. Many factors "feed" this problem, including our fast food culture and the hours we spend in front of the television, computer, and video games.

Our culture is also obsessed with dieting to fight the obesity problem. Commercials and advertisements try to convince us that losing weight will make us look and feel better.

Turn your focus away from looking a certain way or weighing a certain number. Instead focus on being healthy. Vegetarianism shouldn't be considered a weight loss diet. It is a lifestyle choice. And while you don't want to be obese, you can't be underweight as a teenager either. Your cells, muscles, and body tissues need nutrients to function. Your body needs nutrients to grow. Feed your body healthy food.

NUTRIENT NACHOS

Colorful veggies, meat alternatives, good-fat olives, protein-packed cheese, and whole grain tortillas combine a lot of good ingredients into one dish. (Adjust ingredient amounts based on how many people are eating, or how hungry you are!)

Ingredients

texturized vegetable protein

taco seasoning mix

whole grain baked tortilla chips

cheddar cheese, grated

sliced jalapeños

sliced black olives

salsa

guacamole

sour cream

Steps

Cook the texturized protein in a saucepan according to the package directions. Add in the appropriate amount of taco seasoning mix as it cooks.

In the meantime, place tortilla chips on a microwave-safe plate. Sprinkle cheese over the chips. Heat in the microwave on high for about 30 seconds to a minute, or until the cheese melts.

Remove the plate from the microwave. Top your nachos with a spoonful of the taco "meat." Sprinkle with sliced jalapeños and black olives.

Serve with a side of salsa, guacamole, and sour cream for dipping.

CHAPTER FOUR

MAKING THE CUT

IF YOU'VE DECIDED TO SWITCH TO A MEAT-FREE DIET, FIRST FIGURE OUT HOW MUCH MEAT YOU ACTUALLY EAT. It might be helpful to keep a food journal for a week. Count up the times meat makes its ways into your meals. Then you'll have a better sense of how hard or easy it will be to make the transition. You may find that you already eat many vegetarian meals.

You don't have to turn vegetarian overnight. Take it one step at a time. Maybe you can remove beef from your diet first. Then pork, then poultry, and finally fish or shellfish. Jenna decided to give up "anything that could look back at me!"

Have a voice in what's for dinner by offering to help with the shopping.

Or try mapping out a meal schedule for a month. Perhaps the first week, you let yourself eat meat four times. The next week cut down to three. Then two. Then one. In one month, you'll cut out meat altogether.

Steak was the hardest food for Hanako to give up. When she decided to go vegetarian, her family had planned steak for dinner. "So I decided to become a vegetarian a day later," she says.

ALL ABOARD!

Your decision to go vegetarian is going to affect your family too. Your parents or the adults in your life probably do most of the shopping and cooking. They may not be ready to become vegetarians along with you. You'll have to state your case to them.

Know your reasons. Are you becoming a vegetarian because of world hunger, the environment, animals, or your health? The more you've thought about why you want to make this change, the more you'll be able to communicate those reasons to your family and friends. They'll be more likely to support you if they see you've given it a lot of thought.

Your choice to go vegetarian affects your family too.

Be prepared to compromise. Your adults want to be sure you're getting the nutrients you need. And making a separate meal for you might be a lot to ask with everyone's busy schedules. Look for ways to adapt existing meals so they can be served both with and without meat. Perhaps on taco night, your family can serve black beans as a filling in addition to ground beef. If your family has pizza, ask them to make sure half is meatless with lots of veggies instead.

Jenna's parents didn't become vegetarians along with her, but they have benefited from her change of lifestyle. Three or four times a week, the whole family

Organic
Yellow
banana

99¢
LB

Fruits and vegetables
are great sources of
carbohydrates, fiber,
vitamins, and minerals.

eats vegetarian. The other nights, Jenna eats a vegetarian
version of their meal, or makes something different for
herself. By stating her case and sticking up for her cause,
Jenna helped her parents transition to eating less meat too.

AT THE STORE

Take a tour of the grocery store with a new vegetarian view. The
produce section is a vegetarian paradise. If you've decided to eat
milk and eggs, you'll have lots of choices in the dairy section
too. Sometimes stores have health food aisles with all of their
vegetarian alternatives in one place. In the refrigerator and freezer

Be a Label Detective

It would be nice if all vegetarian foods were labeled "vegetarian," but they're not. You have to be on your toes when buying packaged foods. Reading the labels is the best way to check for nonvegetarian ingredients.

For example, canned vegetable soup sounds vegetarian, but canned soups are often made with beef or chicken broth. Most canned beans are vegetarian, but some are traditionally cooked with pork or pork products. Anchovies are a fish that might be used as a flavor for sauces and dressings, such as Caesar dressing or Worcestershire sauce. The more you practice reading labels, the better you'll get at quickly spotting animal products.

You may have to make some tough calls. Your favorite foods may still have some nonvegetarian ingredients. It's up to you.

sections, you'll find meat alternatives and frozen vegetarian meals, such as "fake" chicken, bacon, hot dogs, and ground beef.

The availability of good vegetarian options depends on crops' growing seasons, your location, and the surrounding culture. Grocery stores in some cities may be well stocked with vegetarian items because they serve a lot of customers with varied backgrounds, cultures, and tastes. Your town might have specialty natural food stores, organic grocery stores, and fresh farmers markets. But in some areas, you may be up for a challenge and have limited choices. In ranching states or rural areas, vegetarian options might not be in high demand.

Some vegetarian foods, especially in areas of low demand, may be more expensive than other foods. It can be hard for a family to add extra dollars to their weekly shopping bill. That's why it's good to know your nutrients. A bag of beans is relatively inexpensive. A frozen vegetarian dinner may cost a lot. You may have to get creative with cooking and more involved in meal planning if you want to go meatless.

AT A RESTAURANT

If you decide to go vegetarian, you'll have to look at restaurants through new eyes too. Many restaurants post their menus online. Hop on the computer to read up on them before you go. You can even call a restaurant ahead of time to find out how welcoming they are to vegetarian customers.

If you end up at a restaurant and couldn't do your research first, the menu may have some vegetarian options. Even if most of a restaurant's entrees are meat-centered, the menu may have pizzas, pastas, rice, appetizers, salads, or side dishes that you can make into a meal.

Chefs want to please their customers. Don't be afraid to ask them to adapt a meal for you. They may be able to leave the meat out of a dish easily. Or they might whip up an original vegetarian creation just for you.

Better yet, look for vegetarian restaurants in your area. They are great places to try out food combinations from "expert" vegetarians. You may even get ideas for meals to make at home.

It is often easy to find vegetarian restaurants in cities, where there are a large variety of cultures and tastes.

Try new flavors at a vegetarian restaurant, and get ideas for meals to make at home.

Junk Food Is Still Junk Food

Vegetarian diets have been proven to be healthful. But that's only if you eat the good things your body needs. There are plenty of vegetarian junk foods for sale at the store too. Super-caloric chocolate chip cookies don't have meat in them. But that doesn't mean they're good for you. Your extra-cheesy pizza topped with fried eggplant may be filled with just as much fat as a double hamburger.

And sugar, while it's a carbohydrate that your body can turn into energy, is just empty calories when there are no nutrients attached. A 12-ounce can of grape soda is vegetarian. But the sugar found in a bunch of grapes—that also contains vitamins and fiber—is a lot better for your body.

TRY SOMETHING NEW

For everyone, vegetarian or not, healthy eating means getting your fuel from a variety of sources. Since you were little, parents, teachers, and other adults in your life have probably told you not to be afraid to try something new. Let vegetarianism expand your

Meat Swap

Some companies have created "fake" versions of meat to make it easy to switch.

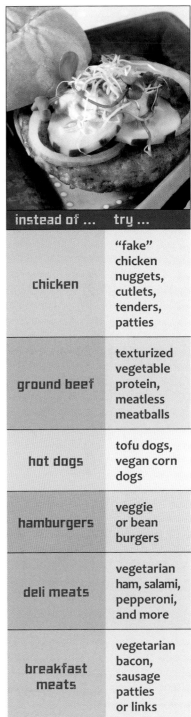

instead of ...	try ...
chicken	"fake" chicken nuggets, cutlets, tenders, patties
ground beef	texturized vegetable protein, meatless meatballs
hot dogs	tofu dogs, vegan corn dogs
hamburgers	veggie or bean burgers
deli meats	vegetarian ham, salami, pepperoni, and more
breakfast meats	vegetarian bacon, sausage patties or links

food horizons. Going vegetarian is a great chance to try foods from other cultures, such as lentil soup, tofu stir fry, and pasta primavera. Use the chance to try star fruits, black-eyed peas, Brussels sprouts, or edemame.

Why not pick up a new skill to go with your new lifestyle? Cooking! Making your own meals is a great chance to take a little more control over your food choices. Bookstores and libraries have shelves of vegetarian cookbooks to spark new meal ideas. Check them out.

Kimberly, a senior who has been a vegetarian since she was 13, has even decided to make vegetarian cooking her career. She takes culinary arts classes at her high school and she's going to continue honing her skills when she graduates. "I'm going to the Culinary Institute of America in the fall," she says. "My best friend and I always talk about opening up our own vegetarian restaurant some day."

Learning to cook is a great way to experiment with new vegetarian meals.

QUINOA TROPICAL TREAT

Try this tasty alternative to a protein-packed breakfast. Quinoa (pronounced keen-wah) looks and acts like a grain, but it's a seed. You can cook it up for breakfast in a way similar to oatmeal. Or you can serve it as a side to a main dish. Enjoy this bowl on a cold winter morning when you want to feel as if you're on a tropical vacation! (hearty serving for one)

Ingredients

½ cup quinoa

½ cup soy milk or fat-free milk

½ cup water

2 tablespoons sweetened flake coconut

½ cup pineapple chunks

2 tablespoons macadamia nuts

Steps

Rinse and drain the quinoa in cold water. Combine the quinoa, milk, and water in a saucepan.

Cover and heat on the stove until just boiling. Then turn down the heat and let simmer for about 10 to 15 minutes, stirring occasionally. You'll know it's done when most of the liquid is absorbed and you see the little "tails" come out of the quinoa seeds.

Place the quinoa in a bowl. Add the coconut, pineapple chunks, and nuts. Stir well. Add extra milk if you like.

UP FOR THE CHALLENGE

YOU'RE LUCKY TO LIVE IN A TIME WHEN VEGETARIANISM HAS BECOME A MORE ACCEPTABLE LIFESTYLE. But if you decide to go vegetarian, you'll still be in the minority. It may be a challenge to have a different outlook from everyone around you. Ashley lives in a small town where "basically everyone hunts and eats a lot of meat," she says. "I feel that I sometimes get criticized for being different."

Support from family members can make the switch a lot easier. That helped Hanako. Her mother was already a vegetarian and does most of the cooking in her family, so it was easy for her to make the transition. But what do you do when you're the only vegetarian in your family? Or one parent is supportive, but the other one isn't? Or everyone thinks you're just going through a phase and that you'll grow out of it?

Sometimes people are critical when they don't understand something. Be ready to answer your critics. Share your reasons for going vegetarian so they know why you made the choice and why it's important to you.

AVOIDING AWKWARD SITUATIONS

You probably know what to expect at meal times at home. But what happens when you go over to a friend's house for dinner?

Don't be shy. It's OK to speak up. Let them know you're a vegetarian before you get there, then leave it up to them. You don't want to surprise or embarrass them at the dinner table when you say, "I can't eat that." Maybe they'll plan a meal that they can adapt for you. Perhaps they'll all go vegetarian for the night. If you can't eat the main meal, maybe you can fill up on a salad or side dish instead.

Jenna's friend's family always makes stromboli when Jenna comes over. To make her feel welcome, they bake one with ham and cheese for them, and a special one for Jenna with cheese and veggies.

Kimberly says that the most festive times of the year are sometimes the toughest. "Holidays are hard," she says, "because the meals are usually centered around meat." No other holiday is as focused on food as Thanksgiving. Serving turkey, gravy, and all the sides is a tradition practiced by many American families. A meal that is supposed to bring family and friends together can sometimes be stressful for a vegetarian. Some hosts don't like to change the way they've prepared their meal for years. So what do you do?

Holiday dinners often have lots of side dishes to choose from, such as salad, vegetables, potatoes, and bread. But sometimes these are prepared with meat ingredients too. You may not want

Even though meat is often the main dish for a holiday, you can enjoy the festivities by contributing something meatless to the meal.

You Don't Have to Go It Alone

It's nice to have support for everything you do. Teams and clubs are places where like-minded people can share ideas, cheer on successes, and comfort in defeats. Deciding to become a vegetarian is a big step. It's nice to have support for this new decision.

If you can't find a vegetarian community in your area, maybe you could start one yourself. Check with your school administrators about how to go about starting a club. Spread the word through your school newspaper or announcements. Perhaps the people you least expected will step up to support you!

to offend your hosts by not eating the feast they spent all morning preparing. At the same time, you want to feel included in the meal and respected for your choices.

Perhaps you can offer to contribute to the holiday feast. Offer to make an alternate main dish with "fake" turkey, or a vegetarian side dish. This way you know you'll have something to eat if the rest of the meal isn't vegetarian. And you'll also be able to show your relatives that vegetarian dishes can be just as tasty as nonvegetarian ones. Perhaps you'll convince some people to try meatless meals more often!

Vegetarian Statistics

How many vegetarians do you know? The *Vegetarian Times* study of 2008 found the following information about vegetarian adults (kids weren't included in the poll, but there are lots of vegetarians under 18).

REASON PEOPLE BECAME VEGETARIAN

health	53%
environmental concerns	47%
animal welfare	54%

PERCENT (0 20 40 60 80 100)

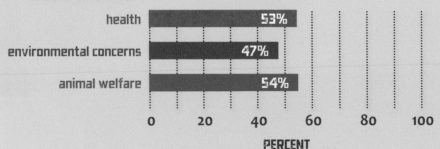

Ages of Vegetarians

42% age 18-34   17.4% over 55

40.7% age 35-54

MAKE A STATEMENT

Going vegetarian means you'll have to spend more time thinking about, planning, and preparing what you eat. Seek out a vegetarian community. Share tips, share recipes, and share support with each other. They'll understand where you're coming from.

Not everyone will agree with your decision. If you live in a community with lots of ranchers, farmers, or hunters where meat is often a topic of conversation, you may feel even more in the minority. The more you know, the better you can argue your case. Hold your own, and don't let others get to you if they don't agree with your views.

Try to find friends in your community who have a similar outlook about food. They will be a good support for you.

Most of all remember that respect goes both ways. If you want people to respect your decision to go vegetarian, you need to respect their decision not to. You can find ways to share your opinions without criticizing their food choices.

Live by example. Show others how happy and healthy vegetarianism makes you feel.

SWEET POTATO MUFFINS

You can convince anyone that vegetarianism is a tasty alternative with this recipe! Eat these muffins for breakfast, pack them for a quick snack, or have them alongside a bowl of soup. (makes one dozen muffins)

Ingredients

1 sweet potato (½ cup mashed)

1 small banana (¼ cup mashed)

½ cup soy milk or fat-free milk

¼ cup vegetable oil

2 tablespoons maple syrup

¼ cup brown sugar

1 cup white flour

¾ cup whole wheat flour

2 teaspoons baking powder

½ teaspoon cinnamon

½ cup walnuts

Steps

Preheat oven to 400°F.

Peel the sweet potato and cut into chunks. Place in a saucepot and add water just to cover the potato chunks. Heat to boiling. Cover and let simmer for about 15 to 20 minutes, or until tender.

Drain and rinse the potatoes under cold water to cool. Place in a bowl. Add the banana, milk, oil, syrup, and sugar. Mash them together until creamy.

Add the flours, cinnamon, baking powder, and nuts. Stir to combine.

Spoon batter into a muffin pan, filling each cup about halfway.

Bake for 15 to 20 minutes, or until a toothpick inserted into center of a muffin comes out clean. Garnish with nuts, if desired.

METRIC CONVERSIONS

TEMPERATURE

degrees Fahrenheit	degrees Celsius
250	120
300	150
350	180
375	190
400	200
425	220

WEIGHT

United States	Metric
1 ounce	30 grams
½ pound	225 grams
1 pound	455 grams

VOLUME

United States	Metric
¼ teaspoon	1.2 milliliters
½ teaspoon	2.5 milliliters
1 teaspoon	5 milliliters
1 tablespoon	15 milliliters
¼ cup	60 milliliters
⅓ cup	80 milliliters
½ cup	120 milliliters
1 cup	240 milliliters
1 quart	1 liter

GLOSSARY

contaminant a substance that causes impurities or pollution

desertification the process of land turning into desert and unusable for animals, plants, and people to live

emission a substance released into the air

fortified containing added nutritional ingredients

groundwater water found in underground chambers; it is tapped for drinking water through wells and springs

irrigate to supply with water

manure animal waste used as fertilizer

nutrient a substance in food that a body needs to grow and function

obese far above normal weight, depending on a person's height, build, gender, and age

organic processed in a more natural way to help conserve the health of land, animals, and crops

pesticide a chemical used to kill insects or small animals

supplement an extra source of a vitamin or mineral

toxin a substance that is harmful or poisonous

undernourished not receiving enough food or nutrients for proper growth

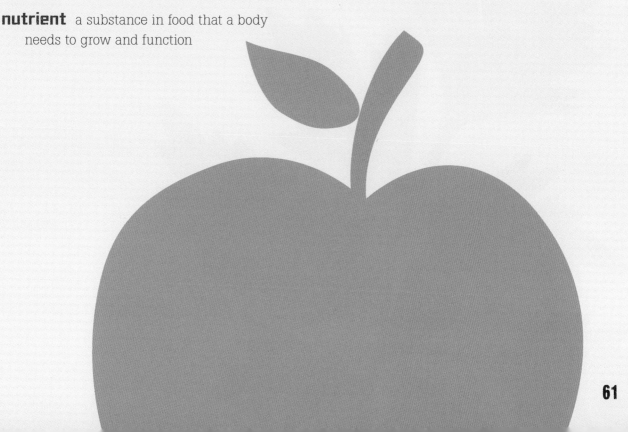

READ MORE

Kneidel, Sally, and Sara Kate Kneidel. *Veggie Revolution: Smart Choices for a Healthy Body and a Healthy Planet.* Golden, Colo.: Fulcrum Publishing, 2005.

Pollan, Michael. *The Omnivore's Dilemma, Young Reader's Edition: The Secrets Behind What You Eat.* New York: Dial, 2009.

Rau, Dana Meachen. *A Teen Guide to Quick, Healthy Snacks.* Mankato, Minn.: Compass Point Books, 2011.

Schlosser, Eric, and Charles Wilson. *Chew on This: Everything You Don't Want to Know about Fast Food.* Boston: Houghton Mifflin Co., 2006.

INTERNET SITES

Use *FactHound* to find Internet sites related to this book. All of the sites on *FactHound* have been researched by our staff.

Here's all you do:

Visit *www.facthound.com*

Type in this code: **9780756545222**

ABOUT THE AUTHOR

Dana Meachen Rau has written more than 300 books for children and teens, including cookbooks that encourage healthy, thoughtful eating. She visits farm stands, tends her garden, and makes meals with her family in Burlington, Connecticut.

INDEX

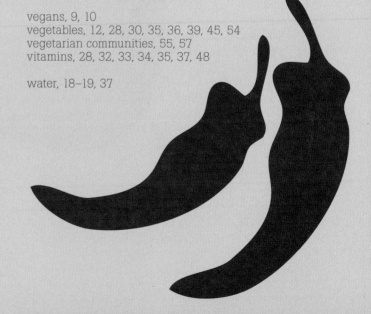